Maths 5-6
Multiply & Divide

Lynn Huggins-Cooper

Contents

Information for parents

This book makes learning fun. The activities are designed to consolidate the learning experienced by 5–6 year olds as part of the National Curriculum. Do not be concerned if your child is working at a higher or lower level than some of the activities. All children develop at their own pace. You know your child and their capabilities best, so be guided by them. If they find something difficult, come back to it later – they may not be ready.

Do not carry out activities that are beyond them, as they will become frustrated. Once the activities become a chore, you will find it difficult to encourage your child to get involved and engage with the book. Instead, fit the activities into your usual day. When you are carrying out the activities in this book, try to make sure your child has quiet time, free from distractions such as the television. Make sure you are relaxed too and not in a hurry or distracted. Give your child your full attention and they will enjoy the 'together time'. If learning is fun, your child will be eager for more!

Sometimes, if your child is tired or has had a long day, they may not want to carry out activities. Do not become anxious about this; they will carry out the work in their own time. If your child needs extra help or support with an activity, do not worry. Children learn and develop at different rates and your child may need extra time to complete a piece of work.

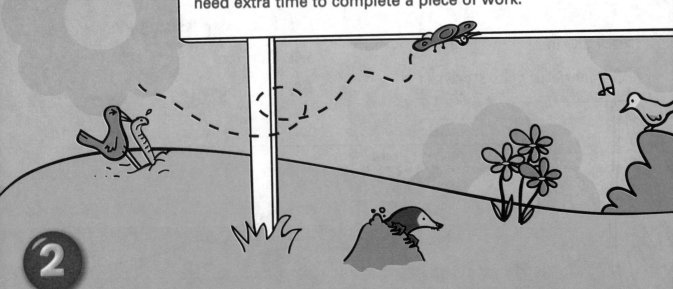

Each double-page spread in the book contains a themed activity for your child to complete, with your support. Parent's notes explain the educational value of these activities and also suggest extension activities to help further your child's learning after the pages have been completed. This will help your child to develop a broader understanding of each concept as it is covered.

Provide your child with a clear place to work, such as their own desk or their own corner of the kitchen table. Give them a set of pencils and crayons in their own pencil case so they feel 'grown up' and prepared to work. Encourage them to do 'little and often' for the most benefit, so they do not get too tired – a day at school can be exhausting!

Look at the pages together and discuss what you can see. Talk about the activity, making sure your child understands exactly what it is they need to do and how they should record their answers. Demonstrate what to do if your child seems unsure. After each spread, help them to check their answers and talk together about what they have learned and whether they found the activity difficult.

Of course, make sure you give your child lots of encouragement and praise, rewarding their efforts as well as their achievements.

Princess' pretty flowers

Princess the pig is adding flowers together.

🌼 + 🌼 + 🌼 + 🌼 = 🌼🌼🌼🌼

$$2 + 2 + 2 + 2 = 8$$

She found an easier way to write the sum: $4 \times 2 = 8$

Help Princess to add together these groups of flowers.

a 🌼 + 🌼 + 🌼 + 🌼 + 🌼 = 🌼🌼🌼🌼🌼

$$2 + 2 + 2 + 2 + 2 = \underline{\qquad}$$

$$5 \times 2 = \underline{\qquad}$$

b 🌼 + 🌼 + 🌼 = 🌼🌼🌼

$$2 + 2 + 2 = \underline{\qquad}$$

$$3 \times 2 = \underline{\qquad}$$

c 🌼 + 🌼 = 🌼🌼

$$2 + 2 = \underline{\qquad}$$

$$2 \times 2 = \underline{\qquad}$$

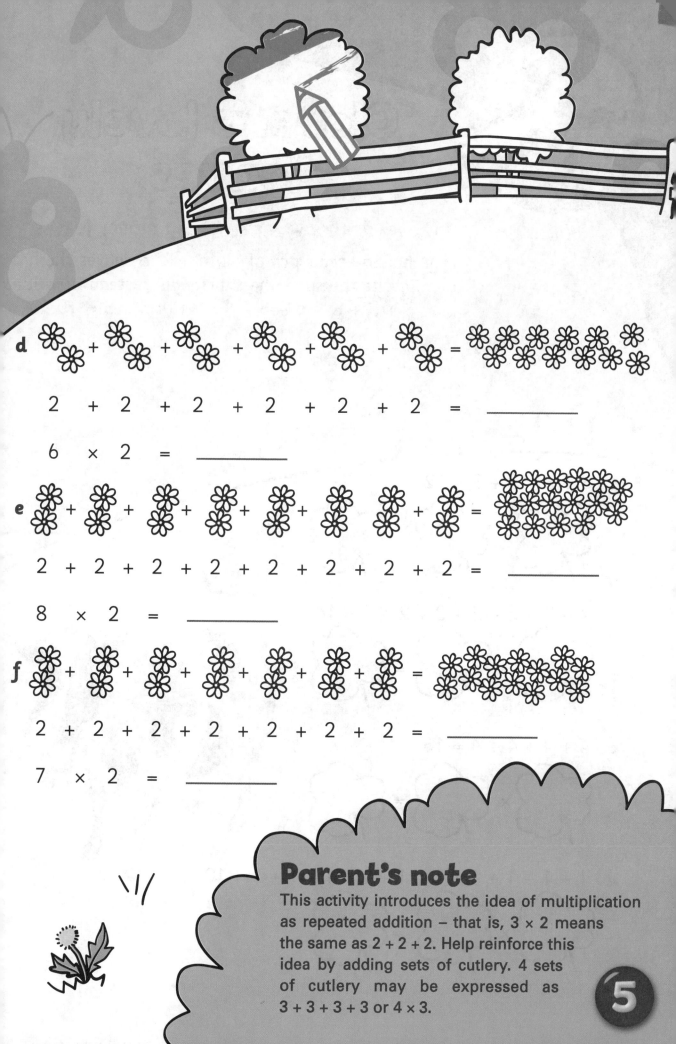

d

$$2 + 2 + 2 + 2 + 2 + 2 = \underline{\hspace{2cm}}$$

$$6 \times 2 = \underline{\hspace{2cm}}$$

e

$$2 + 2 + 2 + 2 + 2 + 2 + 2 + 2 = \underline{\hspace{2cm}}$$

$$8 \times 2 = \underline{\hspace{2cm}}$$

f

$$2 + 2 + 2 + 2 + 2 + 2 + 2 = \underline{\hspace{2cm}}$$

$$7 \times 2 = \underline{\hspace{2cm}}$$

Parent's note

This activity introduces the idea of multiplication as repeated addition – that is, 3 × 2 means the same as 2 + 2 + 2. Help reinforce this idea by adding sets of cutlery. 4 sets of cutlery may be expressed as 3 + 3 + 3 + 3 or 4 × 3.

5

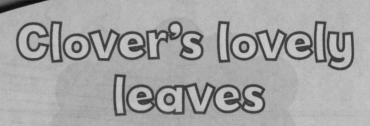

Clover's lovely leaves

Clover the cow is munching clover leaves.

Help her to keep track of all the clover leaves she has eaten. Write the sums the short way. Instead of writing 3 + 3 + 3 + 3 + 3 = 15, write 5 × 3 = 15.

a 3 + 3 + 3 + 3 = 12

⬡ × ⬡ = ⬡

b 2 + 2 + 2 + 2 + 2 + 2 + 2 = 14

⬡ × ⬡ = ⬡

c 4 + 4 + 4 + 4 = 16

⬡ × ⬡ = ⬡

d 1 + 1 + 1 + 1 + 1 + 1 + 1 + 1 + 1 + 1 = 10

⬡ × ⬡ = ⬡

e 10 + 10 + 10 + 10 + 10 + 10 = 60

 ×  =

f 5 + 5 + 5 + 5 + 5 = 25

× =

g 2 + 2 + 2 + 2 + 2 + 2 + 2 + 2 + 2 + 2 = 20

× =

h 10 + 10 + 10 + 10 + 10 + 10 + 10 + 10 = 80

× =

Parent's note

This activity reinforces the idea of multiplication as repeated addition – that is, 4 × 10 means 10 + 10 + 10 + 10. Give your child physical objects to make into equal sets to explore the idea further.

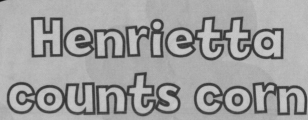

Henrietta counts corn

Henrietta the hen is counting corn. She is using multiplication to make adding up easier.

Help Henrietta to count the corn by completing these sums. Write the answer on the sack.

a +

2 × 4 =

b + + +

4 × 2 =

c + + + + +

6 × 3 =

d + +

3 × 5 =

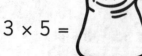

e $\vcenter{}$ + $\vcenter{}$ + $\vcenter{}$

$3 \times 4 =$

f $\vcenter{}$ + $\vcenter{}$ + $\vcenter{}$

$3 \times 10 =$

Parent's note

This activity will help your child to see multiplication as 'sets of'. This makes maths real and solid, rather than just an abstract idea. Arrange toys such as bricks or teddies into equal sets and ask your child to write the matching 'sum' on paper to reinforce the idea.

Sebastian plans a picnic

Sebastian the sheep is planning a picnic with Gus the goat.

Help Sebastian to work out how many of each item of food he needs. Double the numbers so there are enough for Sebastian **and** Gus. Draw the extra things in the baskets, then write the total number in the boxes.

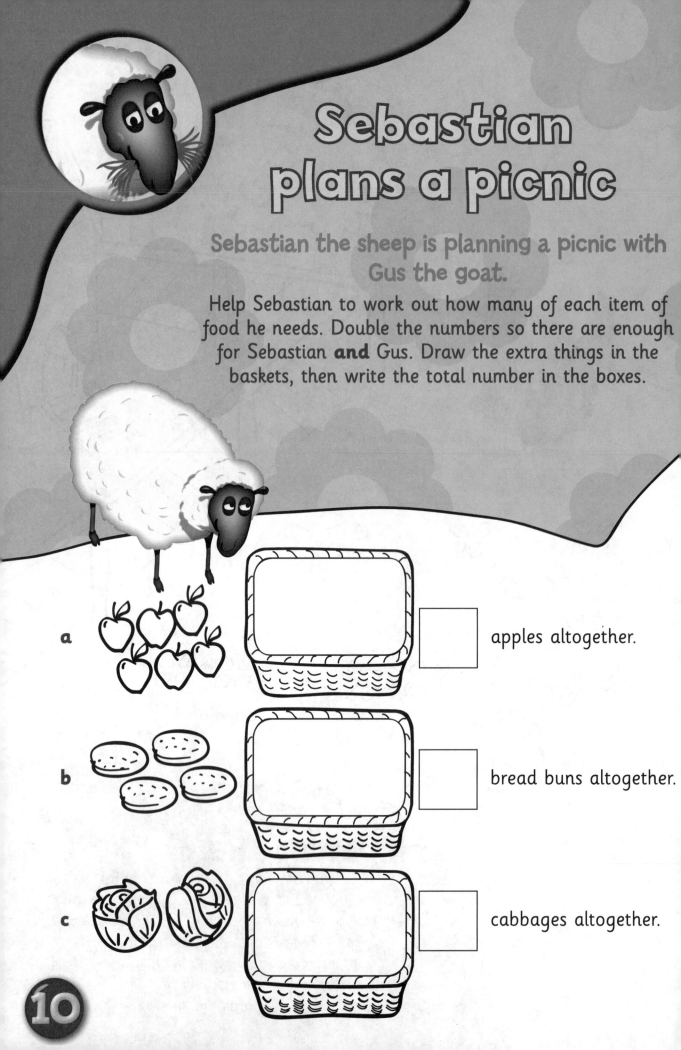

a ☐ apples altogether.

b ☐ bread buns altogether.

c ☐ cabbages altogether.

d oats

bags of oats altogether.

e

potatoes altogether.

Parent's note

This activity will help your child to think about doubling numbers. Practise in a real-life context by working out how many biscuits, grapes, drinks, etc. you need for your family.

11

Fun time!

Look at these two pictures of Henrietta and her chicks.
They look the same – but are they?

There are 12 differences between the pictures.
Draw a circle round each difference you find.

Parent's note

'Spot the difference' activities help to build observational skills and a longer concentration span. You could play the memory game, where your child looks at a tray of objects which is then covered and your child tries to recall them, to further develop these areas.

Terence watches the weeds

Terence the tractor is looking at all the weeds growing in the farmyard. They keep multiplying, so there are more in each patch every day!

Help Terence to work out how many more weeds there will be in each patch. Write the answer in the weed shape, then draw the right number of weeds in the compost sack.

a $1 \times 2 =$

b $6 \times 2 =$

c $2 \times 2 =$

d $5 \times 2 =$

e 7 × 2 =

f 4 × 2 =

Parent's note

This activity introduces your child to simple multiplication. Make some '2× table' cards to help her. Write the question on one side – e.g. '3 × 2', and the answer on the other – '6'. Your child can then test herself using the cards.

15

Candy sorts her toys

Candy the cat is sorting her toys into sets.
Help her by drawing the toys in sets in the boxes below.

a Draw 10 squeaky mice as 2 sets of 5.

c Draw 8 gold bells as 2 sets of 4.

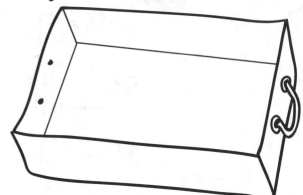

b Draw 10 soft balls as 5 sets of 2.

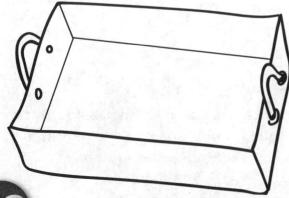

d Draw 12 bouncy balls as 4 sets of 3.

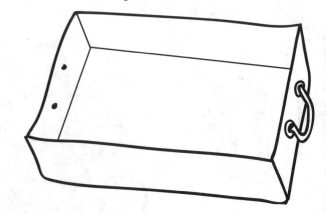

e Draw 8 chewy chicks as 4 sets of 2.

f Draw 6 fluffy bunnies as 2 sets of 3.

Parent's note

This activity explores the idea of multiplication as 'sets of' objects. Play around with real objects, such as shells, to explore this idea further. Make sure your child understands that a number of objects may be arranged into a variety of different sets. 12 objects, for example, can be arranged as 2 sets of 6, 6 sets of 2, 4 sets of 3, 3 sets of 4, etc.

17

Daffodil counts in 5s

Daffodil the dog is stacking her bones in sets of 5. She wants to know how many bones she has altogether.

Help Daffodil by adding the sets of bones together. Write the number in the dog collar.

a    bones altogether.

b 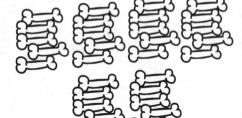  bones altogether.

c 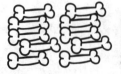    bones altogether.

d    bones altogether.

18

e _____ bones altogether.

f _____ bones altogether.

19

Horace counts in 10s

Horace the horse is looking at his store of apples. There are 10 apples in each box.

Help Horace to work out how many apples he has each time. Write the answer on the hay bale.

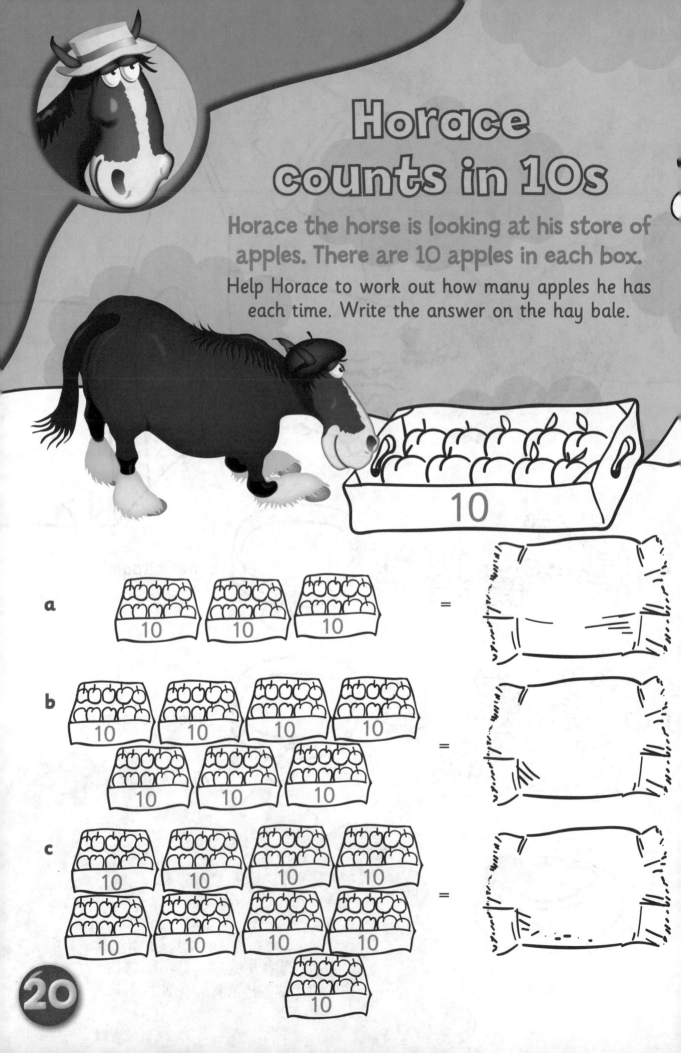

a 10 10 10 =

b 10 10 10 10 10 10 10 =

c 10 10 10 10 10 10 10 10 10 =

d

10 10 10
10 10 10

=

e

10 10 10 10
10 10 10 10

=

f

10 10 10
10 10

=

Parent's note

This activity will help your child to learn about multiples of 10 – the 10× table. Point out that multiples of 10 always end in zero – 10, 20, 30, etc. Encourage your child to make a 'counting in 10s' number line and see how far he can go.

21

Gus sees patterns

Gus the Goat has written some numbers on these walls with chalk. He is looking at the patterns made by the numbers in the 2, 5 and 10 times tables.

Look at the number line that Gus wrote on the wall. Put a cross through the numbers in the 2× table, circle the numbers in the 5× table and tick the numbers in the 10× table.

1	2	3	4	5	6	7	8	9	10
11	12	13	14	15	16	17	18	19	20
21	22	23	24	25	26	27	28	29	30
31	32	33	34	35	36	37	38	39	40
41	42	43	44	45	46	47	48	49	50

51	52	53	54	55	56	57	58	59	60
61	62	63	64	65	66	67	68	69	70
71	72	73	74	75	76	77	78	79	80
81	82	83	84	85	86	87	88	89	90
91	92	93	94	95	96	97	98	99	100

Parent's note

Once these numbers are marked, your child can look at the patterns they make. Look at the way the numbers 0, 2, 4, 6, 8 repeat in the 2× table; that 0 and 5 repeat in the 5× table and that all the numbers in the 10× table end in 0.

Fun time!

Here are the Fun Farmyard friends eating their breakfast. Why don't you colour them in?

Parent's note

Colouring in is not just a time filler. It supports the development of fine motor skills in your child's hands and fingers. These skills will help her to hold pencils and crayons, and this will benefit her writing and drawing skills.

25

Henrietta tells stories

Henrietta the hen is telling number stories to Cheeky, Cheery and Chirpy.

Help them to work out the answers to the number stories. Write the answers on the lines.

a 4 goats had 2 carrots each.

How many carrots altogether?

_____

c 6 cats had 3 fish each.

How many fish altogether?

_____

b 3 horses had a hat each.

How many hats altogether?

_____

d 5 dogs had 2 bones each.

How many bones altogether?

_____

e 8 sheep had 5 apples each.

How many apples altogether?

_____

f 2 cows had 6 bales of hay each.

How many hay bales altogether?

_____

Parent's note

This activity will help your child to see multiplication as a way of solving real-life problems. Encourage her to use multiplication to make totals in shops – 3 chews at 10p each making a total of 30p, etc.

27

Clover and Horace share

Clover the cow is in a good mood. She has decided to share her clover leaves with Horace the horse.

Clover has 18 clover leaves. Share them equally between the two bags. Draw the right number of leaves in each bag.

Horace is very grateful. Now he is sharing his carrots with Clover. Horace has 14 carrots. Share them equally between the two baskets. Draw the right number of carrots in each basket.

Parent's note

This activity introduces division as 'sharing'. Give your child practice by asking him to share out biscuits, fruit, etc.

29

Sebastian has a party

Sebastian the sheep is having a little party. He has lots of party snacks and is sharing them with his friends.

Help Sebastian to share out these snacks equally. Draw the right number of snacks on each animal's tray.

a 4 drinks of water

b 12 lettuces

c 8 handfuls of hay

d 16 carrots

e 20 apples

Sebastian

Clover

Gus

Horace

Parent's note

This activity gives your child practise in 'sharing' – an introduction to division. Encourage him to practise by playing tea parties with his teddies, sharing out cups, saucers, plates, play food, etc.

Cheeky, Cheery and Chirpy share seeds

Henrietta the hen has collected a big bag of seeds for dinner. She is sharing them out between her chicks.

Help Henrietta to share each pile of seeds equally by writing the correct number in each chick's dish.

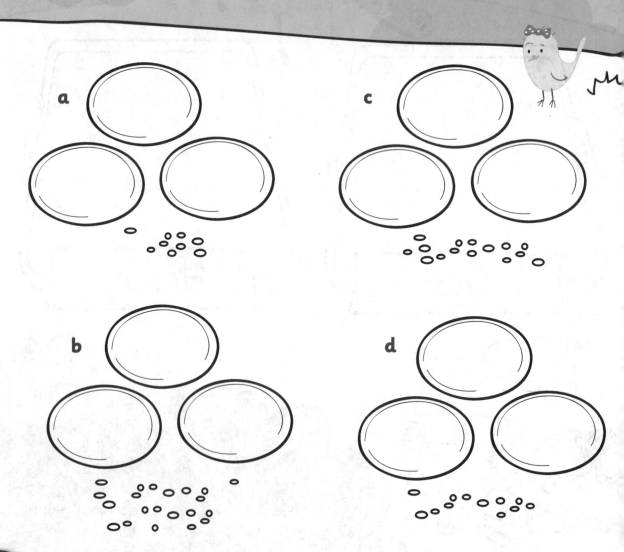

a

b

c

d

e

f

Fun time!

Join the dots to see which Fun Farmyard friend
is standing in the vegetable garden.

Parent's note

Dot-to-dot exercises are fun to do and teach your child about sequencing numbers. Encourage your child to say the numbers as he joins them, to help embed the sequence in his memory.

35

Candy plays with Daffodil

Candy the cat likes playing with Daffodil the dog. She always shares her toys and treats.

Half of each group of things are for Candy and half are for Daffodil. Draw circles to divide each group into two.

37

Daffodil halves numbers

Daffodil the dog thinks halving things is fun!

Help her by halving these numbers. Write the number in the paw prints.

a 20

d 18

b 16

e 10

c 12

f 14

Parent's note

This activity further develops the idea of halving as dividing by 2. Make a set of cards with the numbers 2, 4, 6, 8, 10, 12, 14, 16, 18 and 20. On the reverse side, write the half values, i.e. 1, 2, 3, 4, 5, 6, 7, 8, 9, 10. Your child can use the cards to learn the half values of all the numbers to 20.

Terence goes backwards and forwards

Terence the tractor travels backwards and forwards carrying hay for all the animals. He thinks of sums as he does it, so he doesn't get bored.

Help Terence by filling in the missing numbers.

$3 \times 2 = 6$

$6 \div 2 = 3$

a

$6 \times 2 =$

$12 \div 2 =$

b

$9 \times 2 =$

$18 \div 2 =$

c

$10 \times 2 =$ ☐

$20 \div 2 =$ ☐

d

$7 \times 2 =$ ☐

$14 \div 2 =$ ☐

e

$8 \times 2 =$ ☐

$16 \div 2 =$ ☐

f

$5 \times 2 =$ ☐

$10 \div 2 =$ ☐

Parent's note

This activity will help your child to see that multiplication and division are 'inverses' – that division will 'reverse' multiplication and take you back to the number you started with. Work through the calculations with your child, pointing out that the same numbers occur in the multiplication and division sequence, but in a different order.

41

Gus eats leaves

Gus the goat is always hungry. Now he is eating leaves.

Gus thinks the tastiest leaves are the ones showing numbers that are in the 10× table. Colour in the leaves showing numbers from the 10× table, so Gus can eat them.

42

Parent's note
This activity explores the 10× table. Point out to your child that all the multiples of 10 end in 0.

43

Princess goes shopping

Princess the pig loves shopping! She and her friends are buying food at the market.

Each farmyard friend has some money to spend. Princess has 20p. Candy has 10p. Daffodil has 30p and Sebastian has 16p.

Carrots
2p

Apples
5p

Potatoes
2p

Cabbages
8p

Write the answers on the shopping baskets.

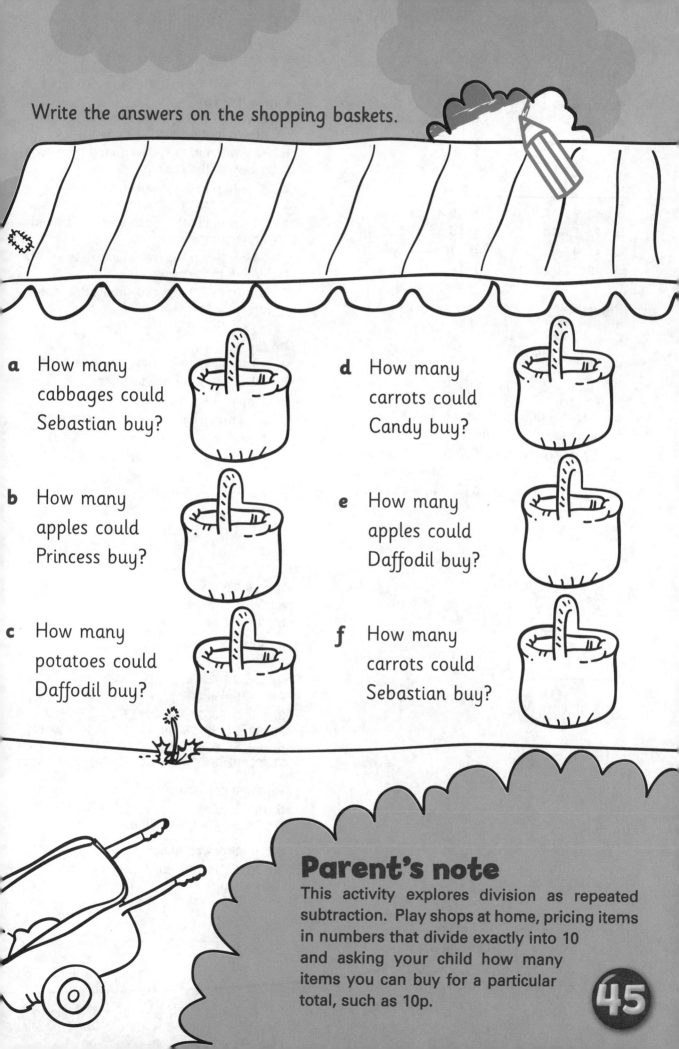

a How many cabbages could Sebastian buy?

b How many apples could Princess buy?

c How many potatoes could Daffodil buy?

d How many carrots could Candy buy?

e How many apples could Daffodil buy?

f How many carrots could Sebastian buy?

Answers

Pages 4–5
a 10, 10
b 6, 6
c 4, 4
d 12, 12
e 16, 16
f 14, 14

Pages 6–7
a 4 × 3 = 12
b 7 × 2 = 14
c 4 × 4 = 16
d 10 × 1 = 10
e 6 × 10 = 60
f 5 × 5 = 25
g 10 × 2 = 20
h 8 × 10 = 80

Pages 8–9
a 8
b 8
c 18
d 15
e 12
f 30

Pages 10–11
a 6 apples drawn, 12 written in the box.
b 4 bread buns drawn, 8 written in the box.
c 2 cabbages drawn, 4 written in the box.
d 1 bag of oats drawn, 2 written in the box.
e 5 potatoes drawn, 10 written in the box.

Pages 12–13

Pages 14–15
a 2 written in the weed shape, 2 weeds drawn in the sack.
b 12 written in the weed shape, 12 weeds drawn in the sack.
c 4 written in the weed shape, 4 weeds drawn in the sack.
d 10 written in the weed shape, 10 weeds drawn in the sack.
e 14 written in the weed shape, 14 weeds drawn in the sack.
f 8 written in the weed shape, 8 weeds drawn in the sack.

Pages 16–17
a 10 squeaky mice drawn as 2 sets of 5.
b 10 soft balls drawn as 5 sets of 2.
c 8 gold bells drawn as 2 sets of 4.
d 12 bouncy balls drawn as 4 sets of 3.
e 8 chewy chicks drawn as 4 sets of 2.
f 6 fluffy bunnies drawn as 2 sets of 3.

Pages 18–19
a 15
b 30
c 20
d 10
e 25
f 35

Pages 20–21
a 30
b 70
c 90
d 60
e 80
f 50

Pages 22–23
All multiples of 2 crossed out.

2, 4, 6, 8, 10, 12, 14, 16, 18, 20, 22, 24, 26, 28, 30, 32, 34, 36, 38, 40, 42, 44, 46, 48, 50, 52, 54, 56, 58, 60, 62, 64, 66, 68, 70, 72, 74, 76, 78, 80, 82, 84, 86, 88, 90, 92, 94, 96, 98, 100

All multiples of 5 circled.

5, 10, 15, 20, 25, 30, 35, 40, 45, 50, 55, 60, 65, 70, 75, 80, 85, 90, 95, 100

All multiples of 10 ticked.

10, 20, 30, 40, 50, 60, 70, 80, 90, 100

Pages 24–25
Picture coloured in as neatly as possible.

Pages 26–27

a 8   d 10
b 3   e 40
c 18   f 12

Pages 28–29
9 clover leaves drawn in each bag.

7 carrots drawn in each basket.

Pages 30–31
A picture on each tray of 1 drink of water,
3 lettuces, 2 handfuls of hay, 4 carrots,
and 5 apples.

Pages 32–33

a 3   d 4
b 7   e 6
c 5   f 8

Pages 34–35
Dots joined to reveal Gus the goat in the
vegetable garden.

Pages 36–37
Many answers are possible, as long as
circles are drawn around half of the objects
in each group.

Pages 38–39

a 10   d 9
b 8   e 5
c 6   f 7

Pages 40–41

a 12, 6   d 14, 7
b 18, 9   e 16, 8
c 20, 10   f 10, 5

Pages 42–43

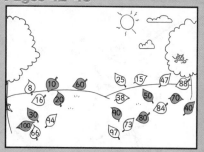

Pages 44–45

a 2   d 5
b 4   e 6
c 15   f 8

Goodbye!

Just colour us in
before you go.